THE
SPIRIT
of
AMERICA

★ ★ ★

THOMAS
KINKADE

THE SPIRIT *of* AMERICA

★ ★ ★

THOMAS KINKADE

WITH CALVIN MILLER

THOMAS NELSON PUBLISHERS
Nashville

This is a work of fiction. The stories recorded in this

book are composite descriptions of many individuals and settings.

Aside from obvious historical Figures, any resemblance to

persons living or dead is purely coincidental.

Printed in the United States of America

Bound in Mexico

2 3 4 5 6 7 - 04 03 02 01 00

THE SPIRIT *of* AMERICA

MY AMERICA

My name is *Jean Pierre Godet*. That's how I used to spell it before I learned to pronounce it the American way: *John Peter Godet*. I was born in Brussels, Belgium, in 1893. There I was christened in St. Michael's Cathedral, and there for the first six years of my life my family used my name in our native tongue. In 1899, near the front end of all I can remember, my father grabbed me by the shoulders and looked into my eyes and nearly shouted, "Jean Pierre, we're going to America!"

America! I thought. *Where is that? How can this be?*

In such a simple phrase was born a new excitement, mostly in my father. But excitement is contagious, and his enthusiasm was soon my own. The next day he came home with a couple of huge steamer trunks and a stack of French francs. He had sold our little farm.

"Jean Pierre," he said, "we cannot take everything we have to America. Do you understand? We must pack in these trunks only what is most essential." And then, as I stared down at the bills in his hands, he broke into laughter and said, "A little land in Belgium will buy a hundred and sixty fine acres of American land."

Papa's words began a century-long adventure. The time we had, itself, is too full to recount, but not the joy of it all. America was God's gift to an idealistic Belgian farmer and his son. And somehow you cannot receive such a gift from God without giving thanks. In fact *God* and *America* are two words that never rise singly in my thoughts. When I think of one, the other comes quickly to mind, and the mortar that holds them together is gratitude.

These events now seem distant, yet I have lived long enough to see the promises of my childhood come to pass. The eight decades since have witnessed their fulfillment.

The twentieth century in a new land! A good land! A land that adopted the orphans of Europe and endowed them with dignity, hope, and pride! But the best part of this gift was time itself—a century of life in America—for in this incredible march of time I became a man. I have,

in growing older, become the head of a family who had the good fortune to seek their futures in a blessed land that rewarded their discipline with abundance.

I have lived longer than I ever dreamed I might. I don't know why. Maybe America is just a good place. Maybe the land itself gives life. But I do know I have lived long enough to observe almost all of the American Century. Yet the God who made me rich with grace would not have me buried in this good soil until I have passed on these memories of all I have seen and felt.

This is the testament of a grateful immigrant, who crossed an ocean and found a destiny. I am an American, and all that is American within me I pass on to you in the hope that we'll find a common celebration in our heritage.

9

TESTAMENT OF AN IMMIGRANT

The first thing that impressed itself in my memory was my father's excitement over leaving Brussels. My mother had died some six years earlier, and her absence from our lives left Papa and me very close. It was hard on both of us after Mama died, and times were hard in Belgium at the turn of the century. America was a land that constantly offended and yet enchanted Europeans. The wealthier Europeans regarded America as a land full of unenlightened and uncultured souls who never would have made it in Europe. But those on the lower rungs of European caste saw the country as a great land in which wonderful, new empires might be won by those who had never owned much in Europe.

My father worked from sunup to sundown on our little Belgian farm. Yet, for all his effort, there never seemed to be much on the table to nourish us. It was understandable that Papa felt trapped where he was. He was ready to dream a better future and the word "America" contained four rich syllables of promise.

"My boy," he said after supper one night, "soon we're going to sail to America, and from there, by God's good grace, into the next century."

"But, Papa," I protested, "what of our farm? What of our family and Uncle Jacques? Will we ever see our friends again?"

"Well," said Papa, "we can write to our family and friends, and as for Uncle Jacques, I've heard that in America the government itself is the uncle . . . Uncle Sam, they call him. He's everybody's good uncle in that world where an ounce of Europe will buy a pound of new life."

Papa squared his shoulders and pointed to the mantel clock. "There is time and land where we're going. Somehow time has gotten old here, Jean Pierre, but they're turning a new century across the Atlantic. If we're going to make a new life we need to go where time is new." Suddenly the confidence in his eyes was his own. "We're not just staking out new territory. We're driving our stake down in a new century.

"I guess Americans have a jar full of time, and they don't need to

measure each spoonful. Really its not merely time that Americans have so much of. It's *tomorrow*. And when you have tomorrow in your heart you never run out of dreaming room. And dreaming is the stuff of hope."

Papa paused a moment. "And there is land too, Jean Pierre—land is so plentiful in America you can stretch your arms any time you want to and never have to worry about crowding your neighbor's space."

That was in January of 1899. We were just about ready to turn the corner into the twentieth century. Nobody knew, I guess, that before that century was over, folks would be calling the twentieth century the "American Century." Nobody except my papa.

MY FIRST IMPRESSIONS
OF AMERICA

W e left Brussels and traveled by train to Paris and from there to Calais. From that post we traveled by ferry across the Channel to Southampton, England.

When we arrived there we immediately realized how England had dominated the last half of the nineteenth century. It is fair to call the nineteenth century the "English Century." But for all that swelling of English pride, it didn't seem so different to me from the rest of Europe in a lot of ways. Anyway, Papa and I were just plain tired of all parts of the Old World. Papa said that England, like Belgium, had been there for a long time. I could see that's why Papa was so fascinated by America. He realized that things don't have value just because they're old. Those old places seemed to make Papa feel even older than he wanted to. He needed a place young enough to make him feel young.

We knew there was a new statue in New York harbor called "Liberty" that was enlightening the world. And we were intrigued by the words lettered in bronze on the plaque at its base.

Give me your tired, your poor . . .

I lift my lamp beside the golden door.

Well, Papa was tired of being tired, and he wanted something more than the hope of not being poor anymore. If there was a door of opportunity he wanted to walk through it.

Papa was no conquistador. He wasn't looking for the fountain of youth or a city of gold. He was willing to work for honest wages and bend his back to make his dreams come true.

He had a picture of an apple farm in Pennsylvania. He had kept it for years, way before he announced that we were going to the New World. I would often see him almost praying over that picture.

But on the day that he told me we were moving, he patted me on the head, took my thin, boyish shoulders, and gently handed me that picture and said, "Look, Jean Pierre, they grow wonderful apples in America!"

"We grow apples in Belgium," I replied rather dully.

"Yes, my boy, but, look at the size of those Pennsylvania apples." He pronounced the word "Pan-seal-van-ya".

"They do look big in the picture, Papa, but you can make a picture of apples any size you like."

"Yes, boy, but those apples are big both inside and out. Where there are big apples there are big trees, and there has to be lots of cider. And where there's cider, there are friends and parties. When harvest-time comes we will share and give thanks. All of this is in America, across the ocean."

He stopped for a moment, then he said, "Son, do you know what Martin Luther once said?"

"What do you mean, Papa?" I asked, unsure of where the conversation was going.

"Luther said, 'Even if I knew the world was ending tomorrow, I would plant an apple tree today.'"

"What does that mean, Papa?" I asked.

"Son," he said, "it means that we're going to plant an apple tree some-where on the other side of the ocean. And before you're old enough to make a pie from that tree, you'll be living in a land where the future is as certain as apple harvest."

Papa was excited, maybe even overwhelmed, at the idea of a new start in a New World. America! I wondered what it would be like.

In Southampton we awaited passage on a small ship that was to take us directly to New York. The boat was called *The New World.* At the time it seemed a name fraught with symbols.

After two days we sailed for America. On the eleventh day at sea, we saw for the first time the coast of Maine. It was rugged—like the Americans themselves. It was all huge rocks and tall trees. But I will never forget two things that declared themselves in Maine: a great lighthouse and a quaint, wooden church. It seemed to me in these two things light was declared—such light that promised safety for either a country or a ship full of hopeful pilgrims.

As we approached that coast in Maine, light poured out, both from the high lantern of the lighthouse and the amber windows of the New England church. That light seemed to say one thing: This is America, where light is customary and freedom is as generous as vision.

All through the long voyage, I remembered that somewhere down in stowage was a carefully wrapped package of grafts from our Belgian apple tree. I knew that long after Papa had spliced those branches, we'd be calling our neighbors in for a big cup of the sweetest cider in the New World.

Well, I was six years old then. When I was sixty that little slip of a Belgian tree was still producing the sweetest apples in America.

Some people call me an idealist. Well that is the way that I know I am an American. America is the only idealistic nation in the world.[3]

WOODROW WILSON

BOSTON COMMONS AND COMMON BOSTONIANS

After we sailed past Maine we docked in Massachusetts. But Boston was the first place Papa and I got off the boat in the New World. It was our first taste of an American city.

Some say that the only thing that keeps Boston from being a European city is the Atlantic. Boston: The place where the long-ago Colonial tea party occurred. It was there where Americans first defined liberty.

Boston Commons was far from common. It was a place for sensing that Americans are the "new proud," in the best sense of the term. And why wouldn't they be proud? In Boston everybody was somebody and trying to be somebody even better. What made Americans great was their intention to make their nation the best nation on earth. In pushing their own individual hungers for excellence, they knew they were making a great nation.

In Boston we ate at a cheap little restaurant. Papa hated extravagance.

There in that tiny little cafe we ordered Boston baked beans and saw firsthand the simplicity that made America rich. Boston was called "Bean Town" for no other reason than that they had figured out how to take a bowl of beans and make them sweeter than the cream pastries of Antwerp.

And I would live long enough to see why even beans could give a city its name and why it would make the city proud. In my lifetime I'd meet Idahoans who felt that way about potatoes and Georgians who felt that way about peaches.

Papa finished his bowl of beans and said what seemed very obvious to my six-year-old mind: "Now, son, that was a bowl of beans!" Who could disagree? Yet I knew what Papa was saying—the beans in Boston were like the picture of those apples in Pennsylvania. Beans were just better in Boston, and apples were superior in Pennsylvania.

There's a kind of delightful brashness about "Yankee competition." Boston was already called "Bean Town," but it was not a cheap way of

trying to be humble. Bostonians baked beans—and they did it right. "Bean Town" was as proud a name as "The Big Apple" is, or the "Windy City." We would soon see that each of the American cities was competitively proud. Each of them believed it was winning the competition in its field.

But Boston wasn't just beans, and New York was more than a big apple. Each of the American cities was a citadel of the human spirit. The cities had great universities. Boston was where you went to get smart. New York was where you went to get rich. Chicago was where you went to get a job. New York made sure America had money. Chicago made sure Americans had dignity. But Boston made sure that Americans would be as smart as any nation in the world.

In Boston Commons I could see firsthand what it was that made Americans very blessed and proud: multiculture! In the Old World people looked alike—too much alike—and people who look the same too often think the same. But Americans were diverse in their appearance,

and that diversity would in time become their richest national asset.

Boston Commons was a place where the only thing held in common was everyone's right to be there. The people we saw in Boston could never be accused of looking alike or thinking alike. Everybody was a package of uniqueness. And out of such individuality a new century was being born.

I didn't know what all this meant at the time, but I knew that as sure as I was eating baked beans in Boston, we'd soon be eating apple pies made in Pennsylvania. And somewhere beyond the beans and pies, would be a whole new world. Our world. Our America.

THE BIG APPLE AND THE BIG PIE

New York City!

We arrived there like most other immigrants who came by the millions. The docks were thronged by hopeful pilgrims lining up before the immigration office. It seemed as though they were all getting married to a new country. The marriages would be many and instantaneous, but then, in America, things happen fast. The immigration officers were the Justices of the Peace. What you did in America was not some tedious rehearsal for life. Everybody who passed under the Statue of Liberty was impatient to claim some empire.

Still, these mass marriages were not so instant that there was no time to see the sights, and there were plenty to see. While you waited for the immigration office to certify your papers you could spend a day or two in Central Park, and you would still have time to take a stroll down Fifth or Sixth Avenue. It was merely exercise, since few immigrants could afford to shop there, and even fewer would have wasted money on a horse cab.

New York was urban—New York was a noisy place—a never-ending symphony of iron rims on brick streets. All we had to do was open the windows of our cheap hotel, and the sounds of the New World flooded in. But in Central Park you could move into a secluded world of trees and gas lamps and solitary benches.

New York was not just one of the colonies that made good. It was not just a state of the Union. New York was a love affair, a state of bliss—a noisy definition that could only be called America. In the Big Apple you knew that America was big and getting bigger.

But New York was not altogether to Papa's liking. Papa never liked crowds and big cities. I could tell by watching him talk to the other immigrants that they were too noisy and hurried for Papa. Finally the citizenship paperwork was done, and we were on our way. But on the way to the train station to leave New York, he turned to me and said, "Now, son,

just you remember New York is right on the East Coast, so it really isn't very far into America. Things'll get better once we're west of town. The apple trees and rich farmland are still ahead of us. Our journey is not yet done."

On the train he seemed to recapture his former mood. Looking through the streaked windows of the railway coach, Papa became animated. "We're in America now, boy. Let's start looking for apple orchards."

When we finally started seeing them, Papa tapped me on the shoulder and smiled. He didn't say anything. I didn't say anything. The apple orchards that whisked by our train window said it all. We were in America! Deep in America and getting deeper into it all the time, into small, wholesome villages filled with good people working to make their country great.

When a great ship cuts through the seas, the waters are always stirred

and troubled. And our ship is moving through troubled new waters toward new and better shores.[5]

LYNDON B. JOHNSON, *State of the Union Address, 1968*

THE PRAYER OF A HAPPY MAN WHO CAME TO LIVE IN
A SMALL TOWN WITH GREAT VALUES

Cedar Falls was our new address! Cedar Falls, USA! A good town with a bustling right to start life over with exactly 391 people including me and Papa. We spent most of the money we got from our land in Belgium on buying our farm in America. But we had enough left over to get us started living our first year. We planted a tiny orchard of apple seedlings and with frost inserted our apple grafts. That spring, neighbors came and helped Papa raise a barn. It wasn't a big barn, but it was a good barn.

A barn raising! The men wielded hammers and saws, and the women cooked pork roasts and berry pies! Looking back on it, the best thing about our first year in America was the warmth of our neighbors. Our new friends had to listen to Papa very closely to pick through his Belgian accent and figure out what he was really saying. But nobody seemed to care that he had an accent because accents were common in Cedar Falls.

It was in the spring when we raised the barn, and most of the food that came to the barn raising came in Ball Mason jars—big jars that were filled with new potatoes—at least they had been new the previous summer when they were cold-packed. Every jar was a clear window of American abundance.

Those big glass "cans," as they called them, were packed with that see-through glory that Americans filled in their earthen fruit cellars. These earthen larders made the snows of winter yield as abundantly as the fields of summer. Once you popped the seal on a glass jar, the aroma of last summer's cast-iron stove was all around you in the air.

Still, the women of Cedar Falls all seemed a little heavy to me—big behind their gingham aprons. But when I pointed this out to Papa, he said, "Well, son, everybody eats well here. Plump is better than sick."

In 1904, when we had been in Cedar Falls for about four years, I came downstairs one night. Papa was at the table reading his Bible, and I overheard him praying a prayer of thanksgiving. There was nothing unusual

31

in Papa saying his prayers. It was his nightly habit. He and God were the best of friends, but he never got so familiar with God that he forgot to be sincere. Papa saw God as the source of all his blessings.

"Dear God, thanks for Cedar Falls and all 391 residents.

"God, You must love me a lot to give me a town of 391 people, and if You don't mind I'd like to thank You for this good piece of farmland two miles outside of town. From there I can watch the rest of the people with a little perspective. I'd like to learn how to be like the best of them and avoid the bad habits of the worst of them. I'd like to pay off my bank mortgage as fast as I can and still have time to sit down with my neighbors at church dinners and cheer the softball team. And if You don't mind, I think I'll keep the mortgage in the family Bible. I'd like to take it out every night when I'm talking to You and let You remind me that I have some debts to pay. And if I store it in the family Bible, I can keep praying over my obligations, while I remember that honesty is the never-ending rehearsal of those who want to be the friends of God and

the 391 people in the good little section of the Kingdom where we live.

"God, there's no use pretending, when there are only 391 people, it's a pleasure to keep on praying. Thank You, God, for America. And best of all, thank You for breaking it all down into bite-sized little places, where clean values and hard work are the two celebrated virtues that can make great big heavens out of pretty little places. And God, bless all those poor unfortunate souls in the Old World who've never been able to thank You, God, for a town of 391 people! Because, God, it's just the right size to remember how important You are and never forget how important the rest of us are either. Amen and Amen."

THE BIG DITCH AND THE AMERICAN WORK ETHIC

Papa was a real fan of Theodore Roosevelt. He never seemed to see what others called the president's imperialist tendencies. Papa saw life as he did. Roosevelt was the very picture of what all Americans could be. Both of them understood that if you worked hard enough you could make a farm in Iowa produce or dig a canal across Panama.

Papa had willingness.

A palindrome developed around the Protestant work ethic in Roosevelt's day: *A man, a plan, a canal, Panama*. A palindrome is one of those sentences that's spelled the same way forward as it is spelled backward. Papa said the confounded phrase over and over again. It always came out a little garbled in his French-tainted speech. Still, he was proud of an American president who could dream that big.

Roosevelt's high test of hard-working Americans had to do with what most Americans called his "big ditch"—the Panama Canal. Well, it was just like Americans to link up those long-separated oceans and then put up a tollbooth on each end. Roosevelt proved to Papa that in America you could pretty much pull off anything if you weren't afraid of work. Roosevelt proved it in Panama, and Papa proved it in Iowa.

Well, it was only natural that Papa, who had just gained his right to vote in 1904, would help elect the man who connected the oceans. He felt good that in his very first election his candidate won. Roosevelt was in office, and Papa was proud.

But Papa somehow was like most people in Cedar Falls. It wasn't merely hard work that built the Panama Canal or made the corn tassel. No sir! The credit for all the really great stuff had to be given to God. God made the world and kept it spinning. To Papa, God was the Author of every wonder that was.

Papa was a natural Christian. We had been Catholics in the Old Country, but there wasn't a Catholic church in Cedar Falls. Papa at first felt this was a shortcoming of America. It was not often that he criticized our new homeland. In fact I can only remember him doing it twice. The first

35

time he criticized the country, he was jammed in with those noisy crowds in the immigration office in New York. The second time was when he downplayed the distinct shortage of cathedrals in Cedar Falls. Those were the only two black marks I ever saw him put on America.

It was after the barn raising that we started going to the Lutheran church. It took Papa a little while to sing some of the Lutheran hymns; I suspect he still harbored some grudges toward Luther for not staying a Catholic. But before long he was singing overloud. His singing was a little nasal and usually caused people to look around to see where the noise was coming from. Still, it blessed Papa, and he could never prevent at least one clear tear from spilling over his rough, weathered face when he started praising God. It usually stayed there for the remainder of the sermon.

I could tell he was slowly changing his mind about Lutherans. It was pretty hard for him to worship God in a Lutheran church and not admire Lutherans. So it came as no surprise to me when one day he sat me down in a chair, picked up his Bible, and preached me one of his short but serious sermons.

"Son," he said, "I've made up my mind to be a Lutheran."

And so Papa was baptized and took his place among the rough-skinned, weather-chapped farmers of Cedar Falls. He never tired of church. He and most of the other farmers lived their faith in God, but they never spent a lot of time talking about Him. They did attend church regularly, and it was pretty clear that they saw God as the Giver of rain and the Grower of grain.

I think the hymn that Papa sang loudest was "Harvest Home." It was the "farmer's hymn" he said. It must have been, for he never failed to sing it overloud every Thanksgiving.

First the blade and then the ear,
Then the full corn shall appear,
God of Harvest, grant that we,
Wholesome grain and pure may be.

In this hymn Papa mixed Lutheranism and farming together.

Everybody seemed to have some special gift to give to the church—something they weren't required to do, but something they did out of the goodness of their hearts. Papa became the steeple keeper. He never was afraid of heights, and so he could lash a rope around his waist and caulk and paint without fear.

"Jean Pierre, when I'm hanging off that steeple I can nearly see God, and I can for sure see our farm. You know, Jean Pierre, a steeple is a finger pointing to God. God's the Author of everything good, boy. He gave me you, and He gave me this farm, and He made me a part of the church and gave me the Lord's love to share."

It was one of the most religious things I ever heard Papa say. But I knew how he felt about God. Anybody could see that. He once told me, "Jean Pierre, some people have only a little love for God and spend a lot of time talking about it. There are others who have a lot of love for God but keep it more to themselves."

Generally Papa was in the latter category.

Thomas Kinkade

N E I G H B O R S ~
INTERRUPTABLE AMERICANS

When I was twenty years old it seemed pretty certain that the world was building for a big war. Most Americans were hoping we could avoid it, but it looked for sure like it was coming. You could sense that America was a big family, and, like all families, we all felt that if we could avoid war we should. But we all agreed that if it had to come, nobody would fight for their farms and families like Americans would fight. It was about that time in my life that I discovered the word "neighbor". I guess I came to realize that everyone I knew felt like family. Papa was in his late forties now, and it was pretty clear that he had never gotten over Mama's death enough to marry again. Still, he never ceased to be a neighbor, and neighbors were for Papa and me a kind of extended family. Neighbors were . . . well, they were neighborly.

In 1913 when people said, "Stop in and have coffee," or "Drop by and see us," they really meant it. There was never so much going on in anybody's world that they couldn't stop and make their world wider for the moment. Their interruptions were their lives.

Besides nobody ever just stopped by for coffee. Every happenstance "stop-by" was to see how everybody else's private worlds were matching up with their own.

But the best things that we did for each other were to apply healing to the hurts we all felt just from the pain of living. In a neighbor's house you could cry a little while they listened. You could ask what they would do or would have done in a particular situation.

We had a little bit of healing that we offered with every oatmeal cookie.

Neighbors were doctors with good, workable homespun remedies.

Neighbors were a place to borrow vanilla.

Neighbors were free advice and a place to trade recipes.

Neighbors were an altar, where you could take your hurts and find prayer—often on the spot—for problems that had no solution except prayer.

Neighbors made quilts together while they made up their plans

for the next day.

In short, neighbors knew the art of stopping. Somehow in the course of America's development the art of stopping would be lost. But Americans perfected it originally. They could stop and later remember where it was they stopped. They made a mental note of what they were doing and knew exactly where they needed to start again once they stopped stopping.

They were busy people. But they understood that when you're too busy to stop you've given away your right to be a neighbor. It's a bad right to abandon because you just never know when you're going to have to interrupt someone else, because the art of being human is the science of give-and-take.

Neighbors seemed to remember what Jesus had to say about it: When asked, "What is the great commandment?" Jesus replied, "Love the LORD your God with all your heart, soul, with all your strength, and with all your mind" (Matt. 22:37). Jesus went on to say "This is the first and great commandment. And the second is like it: "You shall love your neighbor as yourself." (Matt 27:38-39) Jesus must have known that neighbors met needs like

the good Samaritan, or good Pennsylvanians, or good Michiganders. Papa always felt that good Americans were by definition good neighbors.

Well, we had a bonfire over at the Cantrells on Friday after Woodrow Wilson made his declaration of war. It was kind of somber in some ways. We roasted a whole bunch of home-cased sausages—the Brunts had just butchered, so everything was fresh. Papa brought a barrel of apples, and a number, three washtub so the kids would be able to bob for apples, while we grown-ups discussed what the coming war meant.

The smell of leaves and dry bark exhilarated the senses, and most of the evening was pleasant. Papa was very quiet the whole evening. I knew that he didn't want me to go to war. "Just like those Germans to export their misery," he said to me, but quietly so as not to offend the Brunts; after all, it was their pig we were eating. Besides it was the Brunts who had learned how to make their sausages and schnitzels in the very country that had set all of Europe in an uproar, and now America as well.

We walked together toward the huge crock of lemonade that sat on the

table near the trays of fried chicken and the Brunts' pork sausages. "Jean Pierre, you'll probably have to go, but you remember to keep your head down. You're all I got. I'm gonna pray for you, my boy, every night. But I want you to come back, do you hear me?"

I nodded.

"I'm gonna pray, but you gotta keep your head down, do you hear me?"

I nodded again.

There were lots of flags and patriotic crepe draped along the tables of abundance. I felt a little pain in the pit of my stomach. It wasn't the sausages. It was my love for my father.

I passed by the rhubarb pies that night; so did Papa.

In less than six weeks I was off to boot camp. I was in the infantry, and I fought as hard as I could. I fought not only for America but also because of an aging man with a good farm and an apple orchard. For the next eighteen months of my life, I knew he was praying, and I worked hard at keeping my head down.

THERE'S A CHURCH IN THE VALLEY BY THE WILDWOOD

By the time I got back from World War I, I realized—perhaps for the first time—that Papa was getting older. He was in his fifties now, and I noticed something of a change in him. Papa had, of course, always loved God and our little Lutheran church even though it was with some reluctance at first that he had become a Lutheran. But that initial reluctance had, across the years, become a deep commitment. Beloved friends told me later, "While you were overseas, he never missed a Sunday in church praying for you."

"Son," he once said to me, "it seems like as America gets bigger, so do her churches. And there is nothing wrong with big churches. In fact when anything grows it's usually a sign of health. But there is nothing wrong with little churches in towns just like ours either."

I think Papa was right. Our modest parish seemed to thrive on the kind of quiet godliness that took God's love seriously. We sang too! There's something great about people who know each other singing in front of each other. Singing wasn't just for the people who were good at it so those who weren't could listen. Singing was a way of life. When you sang, you understood God's point of view better and you knew that what made life big was learning to worship Him.

As we sang we all sensed that this worship also tended our hearts and any troubles we had during the week. Together in the presence of God like that, men like my papa tended to forget there had been three dry seasons in a row, and the banker—the nasal tenor on row three—forgot that he might have to foreclose, but the louder he sang the more he understood that all the farmers needed was a little rain. And as he sang they all gathered the courage to believe the rain would come in time.

But the best part of our thanksgiving for the years following the war was that I was one of those Johnnys that came marching home. God was given all the credit for my safe return. I believed that it was surely Papa's prayers that had brought me back safe and sound.

In 1922, Papa painted the steeple for the last time. He had to admit

45

that while the steeple was still the finger pointing to God, the finger seemed to be getting longer and he was getting farther and farther from the ground. I spent some time watching him caulk and paint that steeple for the last time. It seemed like he was throwing his whole weight into his back strap. He just leaned back and took his last, high-altitude look at Cedar Falls, and he could see his farm in the distance.

It would be my farm when he was gone, and he spent much of his last years teaching me how to take care of it. I listened, because I had vowed that this little quarter section of America that he so loved were all God's acres. But his surveying the whole of it from the steeple gave me a glimpse of what it meant to survey his part of America from a church steeple.

I never much cared for heights, so I never tried to take up where Papa left off on that steeple. But I tried to remember him as I saw him the last time, seeing all he could and loving all he saw. The following Sunday he accepted the accolades everyone gave him for the new coat of paint on the steeple. We sang heartily that Sunday, just before the preacher preached. We liked our preacher. He was so against sin, and it always seemed to us that he had the right to preach against it since he probably didn't do it as much as the rest of us. So we listened closely when he told us all that we were sinners and we ought to try and quit. On Sundays, right after one of those good sermons, we actually felt like we could quit it. But by Wednesday we found we needed another if we were going to quit for good.

In our little church we knew who was missing from week to week and whether they were mad or sick. If they were mad, we could probably send them a cake, and if they were sick, we'd take them a pot of soup.

One of my favorite hymns went:

There's a church in the valley by the wildwood,
No lovelier spot in the dale;
No place is so dear to my childhood
As the little brown church in the vale.

The hymn didn't mention God much, but it sure was how we felt about the place where we all met to worship Him.

47

Our purpose is to cultivate in the largest possible number of our future citizens

an appreciation of both the responsibilities and benefits which come to them because they are Americans and are free.[9]

JAMES BRYANT CONANT, *Annual Report to the Board of Overseers*, Harvard University

MAIN STREET

I married in 1923, when I was thirty. Most people thought it was about time. Some remarked that Papa was "a crusty old bachelor" raising "a crusty young bachelor," but he had never remarried because he had just never found a woman who measured up to my mother. And I . . . well, I had a lot of things to do helping Papa make his way in America. Papa, like most Americans, lived by a collection of proverbs, one of which was "marry in haste and repent at leisure." So I married at thirty and found he was right.

I married Hildegard Wilhelm, who was the best of the Wilhelm girls. Papa noted, "She's a good Lutheran girl." He never thought it through, but I'm sure he couldn't recollect having met a bad Lutheran girl anyway. She was seven years younger than me but Papa allowed that when you waited as long as I had waited to marry, the best ones would be younger since the older ones were those who went "unpicked" during the picking season.

Hildegard Godet! A German first name and a French last name, but American all the way through.

It wasn't long before Hildegard and I had a couple of little boys, and not much too longer after that our family outings were our Saturday night trip to town. Everybody did it—it was hard to find a place to park your Model "T" because things got so congested. Lots of shiny, new three-hundred-dollar Fords parked all up and down Main Street. Cars hadn't gone into colors yet. They were all black. Henry Ford saw to that. He had told the public pretty clearly, "You can have any color of car you want as long as it's black."

The nice thing about Main Street was that it ran right through town. The idea of bypasses had not occurred to anyone yet. Why would you want to bypass the center of town, anyway? The center of town was where everything happened. It was where you went to people watch. The same people came to town and parked their black Fords in the same place every week. Why? Well, every week they did different things. You could tell how they spent their egg money by what they were

wearing. The married women could also keep their eyes on the young widows, just to be sure they kept their places. And who was the Jones girl dating now? The blacksmith was walking a little funny for it to be so early on Saturday evening. It was hard to understand how his family put up with him.

If you parked your car just right on Main Street you could keep a watch who went into the Bijou. Fortunately movies hadn't started talking yet, so nobody ever said anything bad your kids could pick up. Everybody used lye soap to clean their clothes and wash their kids' mouths out when their mouths filled up with anything you couldn't repeat.

I guess the thing I liked best about Main Street was that you could see the church and the courthouse both at the same time. It would be a long time before I started hearing Americans say you shouldn't try to mix faith and government. In Cedar Falls we believed they went so well together that neither of them was much good without the other. We sang "America the Beautiful" right in church. It never occurred to

us that this could be wrong.

That was 1926.

That was a good time!

Main Street was America.

Nothing much could be wrong in a town full of black Fords and a high school band.

Somehow you felt if you could see the courthouse, all was right with the world. If there was a town square, a town seemed to have square values. If you could see the flag flying, the wind was just right and the weather would be fair.

THE HOUSE

We built our first house in 1927. It had all the latest conveniences: a tin-lined coal bin and a cistern pump right on the sink. Best of all, it had wires between the studs and two-pronged plug outlets in the walls. Those new-fangled incandescent lightbulbs were too bright to look at most of the time. They were talking about eliminating the push-pedal Model "T" Fords with the swanky, new Model "A," and our new house had a garage to put it in whenever they came out.

I built Hildegard a fruit cellar inside the house, concrete plastered too. Hildegard had once met a bull snake in our earthen cellar. She protested the snake and said she had no intention of letting it stay in the cellar. I told her that God had created snakes to keep fruit cellars free of mice. But she reckoned that God had created neither mice nor snakes. She convinced me that it was the will of God to have a cellar entrance inside the kitchen with concrete walls.

Hardwood floors, a claw-foot bathtub, a coat closet off the front hall, and an electrified chandelier over the dining room table: These were all things that Hildy thought a house ought to have.

She told me that she wanted two chimneys so that she could have a fireplace in the bedroom.

"What good would that do?" I asked.

"Good! I'll tell you what good: It's romantic to have a low fire in the main bedroom, that's what!"

"Do you know how much that kind of romance costs?" I asked her. Then I reminded her how expensive chimney bricks were in Cedar Falls. She reckoned that if I had wanted to put a stove and chimney in my work shed, I'd be able to afford the bricks. So I told her I'd build a chimney for our bedroom but it would be a bit smaller and somewhat shorter than the main chimney.

"You build it high enough that it draws good. I don't want my linens to smell smoky in the winter. Besides, romance and a smoky

fireplace don't go together."

So we had two chimneys on our house and a flagstone walkway, along with a double-lattice rose arch and a post lamp. It was a nice house.

But the best part of the house was Hildegard herself. It's a woman that makes a house a home. Hildegard was the best of women and mighty slow to see that ten brick chimneys can't sanctify wood and stone and oak wood floors.

The American woman! It is she who really served to make America. Alexis de Tocqueville once remarked, "If I were asked . . . to what the singular prosperity and growing strength of the American People ought mainly to be attributed, I should reply: To the superiority of their women."

Maybe Hildegard was special mostly to me, and yet I could see in her the qualities that were common to this wonderful and undeclared sisterhood of American women. The nation came to be around their industry and thrift. They ordered life into the future just by doing the simplest of domestic things: home canning, baking, cleaning sheets, and stuffing sausage casings. But they did so much more than domestic things: They could and did help with the plowing, with a kind of grace that never injured their femininity. But they also defined propriety in a generation not far removed from the frontier. They cared about that wonderful American art: reading. Schools were their passion—how they should be built, how they should teach, and what the curriculum should be.

In Hildegard I could see what William Ross Wallace meant when he said of women:

All true trophies of the ages

Are from mother love impearled;

For the hand that rocks the cradle

Is the hand that rules the world.

But best of all virtues was the keeping of the home. Many a night when I came in from the field late I would see the light spilling generously from the hearth, and I would thank God for a woman who made ordinary wood and brick the center of all things wonderful in my life.

I never saw the house without feeling a welling up of thanksgiving to the Lord. A farmer can't help being thankful for the good land and a good, God-fearing woman and for the privilege of living in America where every value and dream is rooted in the home. There at home I remembered the words of Joshua,

> *Now, therefore, fear the LORD, serve Him in sincerity and in truth . . . And if it seems evil to you to serve the LORD, choose for yourselves this day whom you will serve . . . But as for me and my house, we will serve the LORD.*
> (Josh. 24:14–15)

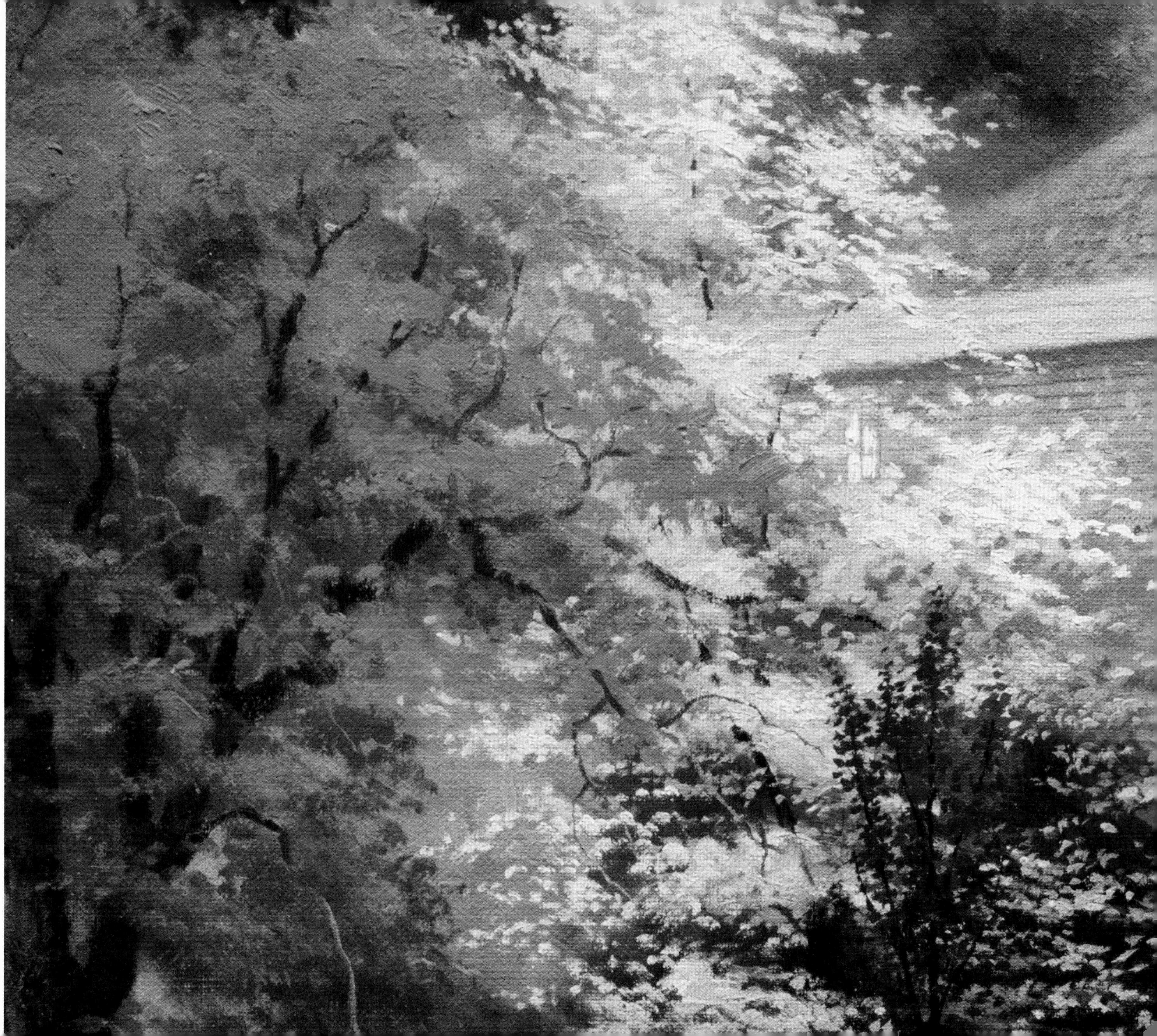

THE PINNACLE OF ACHIEVEMENT

Main Street was cheap entertainment after the stock market crashed in New York on October 29, 1929. "Black Tuesday" they called the day. America for the first time became the "Brother-Can-You-Spare-a-Dime" society. Those were tough years. We counted the eggs on the Godet farm and made sure we didn't drop any of them on the way to the creamery.

Nothing cost much in 1929, but nothing was affordable either. The America I had discovered in 1900 was growing. But it was not just Americans coming first to conquer the wilderness that made the country great. Americans were the creative inventors of a whole new way of life.

I was only ten when I first heard that the Wright brothers had flown their simple airplane at Kitty Hawk, North Carolina. At the time I—like a lot of Americans—thought nothing much would ever come of it. Papa was sure that if God wanted the Wright brothers to fly He wouldn't have made them bicycle repairmen. But the whole event seemed to set the world abuzz with a new kind of imagination. It was who the Wright brothers were that most fascinated me; if bicycle repairmen could attract national attention, this had to be America. America was obviously a place where anybody could just up and try anything.

Well, just as the Great Depression looked like it was easing back, a man named Lindbergh put a little creativity back into the sagging American Spirit. I was just over forty and Papa was in his sixties when a young aviator, whom history would call the "Lone Eagle," flew his airplane, the *Spirit of St. Louis*, across the Atlantic, landing in France. It was a curious flight that ended in darkness with the good people of Paris shining their automobile lights on the runway so he could land on that primitive strip that later would become Orly Airfield.

Papa thought it admirable that the young aviator made it all the way. Still, he allowed "nobody would ever get him up in one of those things."

When I was just over seventy, and Papa was in the churchyard, Neil

Armstrong took his "one small step for man, one giant leap for mankind," stepping onto the moon. Sometimes it is impossible to measure the majestic things a single lifetime can witness. But Americans had a hurry-up view of the future. And the Wright brothers could never know that when they glided off a grassy runway in North Carolina that their flight, primitive as it was, would in time connect to the triumph of a silver-suited American who later stepped onto the moon.

It seemed to me that as airplanes traveled fast, soon cars were going fast. Before long, people started walking fast and driving fast, and soon they just went so fast they didn't seem to have time to stop and say "hello".

At church we had our last dinner on the grounds somewhere in the late sixties. People had quit making lemonade and were just making Kool-Aid on the spot. They were buying their fried chicken from the restaurant, and, while it was good, it just wasn't as good as it used to be.

Times were changing. I missed the world I saw passing away.

Every time I looked up at the church spire, I missed Papa. After his passing, the church steeple never fared well. The steeple tin was always peeling, and the whole thing was just too yellow to point to God very well. Somehow I wanted to slow the world down, but it was hard to slow it down when the horsepower kept going up. The changes were never-ending.

In a world where everything went faster and the good old days were forever receding, I was learning a great truth: A lifetime in America makes keeping your eyes open worthwhile.

AN AMERICAN CHRISTMAS

I guess if ever there was a Christmas that could be called an American Christmas, it was 1941. Just as people were unpacking their nativity sets, Japanese Zeroes attacked the American fleet in Hawaii. Eleven hundred American seamen sank to the bottom of the harbor. Their silent, watery entombment scarred America forever. President Roosevelt declared war, making that December a time that would live in infamy.

Odd as it may sound, there were none who stood against the war. If war can ever be said to be good, this was indeed a "good war." Although suffering and death can never be a benediction on Christmas, this was still a blessed season. The truth is that the lights were a little brighter that Christmas because the eyes of Americans were washed with tears. They had to sing "Joy to the World" fully aware that the world was in pain.

I had two sons that Christmas, and I knew that in the next few months they would likely be called up to take a stand for liberty. We Lutherans were deeply religious, but we believed that peace on earth would have to be purchased with great courage. Christ had, by His Own supreme sacrifice, purchased peace for all who would have it now. Americans also would buy peace with blood.

The purchase of freedom would require that courage become the currency of liberty in places like Bataan, Corregidor, and Iwo Jima. Yet when the dying was done, the world would be safe again for democracy.

But in 1941, for one waiting moment it was Christmas. How we worshiped Christ that Christmas! The dread of war wrote togetherness into every American family and hung a wreath of joy over every hearth. It was the last grand noel before the foxhole Christmases began in 1942.

The Christmases of the forties were as filled with hope as Christmas could be. Mince pies were English in origin, but nobody could make mincemeat like the women of Cedar Falls. Their pies set

the world standard: Crisp, sugar shells that were swollen with hot, dark currents and sweet pork.

Pumpkin too. We grew enough pumpkin in our slough down under the plank bridge to furnish pies to the entire Mississippi Valley. Cranberries came in on the train from Maine, and good old Iowa turkeys were ready for the roaster by the time the cranberries got there. Hildegard spiced ten gallons of cider every year and mulled it with cinnamon sticks on our new kerosene range.

It didn't always snow by Christmas, but when it did, people crowded their way into the Christmas Eve services. I took the Bible out and read it to Hildegard and the boys, just so the fear of the coming war wouldn't erase the promise of the angels. We had electricity now, but Christmas was a time for candles and carols. We sang and prayed away our fears. Perched on the edge of war we had too much faith in God to be paralyzed by fear.

We gathered that Christmas Eve and sang as we never had before:

Hail the heaven-born Prince of Peace!

Hail the Sun of Righteousness!

Light and life to all He brings,

Risen with healing in His wings . . .

Hark! The Herald angels sing,

"Glory to the new-born King."

Let every man honor and love the land of his birth and the race from which he springs and keep their memory green.[13]

HENRY CABOT LODGE, *The Day We Celebrate*

INDEPENDENCE DAY

If the twentieth century is to be called the American Century, surely the fifties must be called the American decade. It was the fifties that exuded the triumph of a culture that shouted to all the world, "Look, I am America. Look upon my vast achievements and concede—America owns a place among the great nations."

I have lived through nearly eight of the nation's growing decades, and I've never seen anything that could match the spirit of the fifties. The twentieth century has seen fourteen presidents come and go. Some were good, some were better, and one or two were hard on America's sense of integrity. All of them—before they were elected—promised that after they were elected they would make America a better place. Each had his attendant programs and slogans. Teddy Roosevelt spoke softly and carried a big stick. Woodrow Wilson wanted to make the world "safe for democracy." Herbert Hoover promised to put "a chicken in every pot." Most of the voters in 1952 decided they liked Ike.

By the fifties, America chose to forget how She once fought her way through the horrible years of the Depression. The rigors of the Watergate scandal and the national debilitation of Vietnam were still unseen in the distant future. America was a growing, expanding nation. She was proud of her great past. Independence Day was never a holiday her citizens could take lightly. In the fifties July the Fourth reigned over a thousand, thousand parks where bands played "Hail Columbia," and fireworks roared out over marching bands playing "The Stars and Stripes Forever!"

The fifties were unquestionably the great years—the years of a burgeoning self-confidence. We had, after all, won a great war in two theaters of operation. Nearly two hundred years after her inception, America was still proud to be America. Main Street was still Main Street. While the USA had become the most powerful nation on earth, she still preferred to think of herself as a small-town place where morality was large and opportunities were great. We were the proud culture of

bobby-soxers, ponytails, rear-finned autos, and sha-boom music. One country-western singer announced that he was proud to be an "Okie from Muskogee." Everybody was proud of being from somewhere it seemed.

The fifties was the era when Americans loved America. The words of Steven Vincent Benét were at last a prophecy:

I have fallen in love with American names,

The Sharp names that never get fat,

The snakeskin titles of mining claims,

The Plumed War-bonnet of Medicine hat,

Tucson and Deadwood and Lost Mule Flat."[14]

But for the first time in my life the fifties presented me with grandsons, and Papa, rounding the corner into his eighties now, had great-grandsons. Papa was wiry and thin and full of stories of scything grain in Belgium or jacking steeples in Cedar Falls.

That was what Papa gave his great-grandsons.

What his great-grandsons gave him was Little League baseball. The fifties were just ahead of the time when a lot of kids would be playing soccer. But we Godets would take the boys first to the ball game and then to one of those newfangled Dairy Queens for ice cream.

Papa used to worry me, working himself up so about the outcome of those games. I'd encourage him to simmer down, but he never simmered down. He loved the dust and display of a long slide into home. He'd stand up and watch every pop fly his "two little men" would hit. But best of all he loved to watch their thin, little arms field the ball back to the infield.

It was fun for me to watch Papa grow old in America. He had gradually become a spectator and philosopher in the art of being an American. He once made America happen. Now he watched America happening. There was no better place to see America than from the short, hard bleachers behind home plate. Somehow America was baseball. It was what children did to become men—to take their own firm stand for democracy.

So when "The Star-spangled Banner" died out and people yelled "Play ball!" America came to life before your very eyes. Once I even heard Papa shout, "Kill the ump!" No ump ever was killed. It was just the way Americans had of reminding everyone that they were accountable for fair play.

Ice cream was the gentle way Americans got together to forget that they had perhaps been a little overheated about their children in the Little League game they had just finished.

It was the way Americans atoned for taking themselves too seriously. We usually invited the ump to come, just so he'd know there was really nothing to the untimely death we had just wished upon him. Just to make sure there were no hard feelings, Papa usually sat by him in church.

THE GOLDEN GATE DOORWAY

Not everybody in the world was looking West to find a land of opportunity. There were a great many world-weary people looking East early in the twentieth century. San Francisco became for the Asians what New York City had been for the Europeans. None of us could know at the beginning of the century what would become apparent by the end of the century: Just as New York held hands with Europe during the nineteenth century, the West Coast of America would hold hands with the Pacific Rim countries in the twentieth. In the latter half of the twentieth century, America was to discover there was not so much to be gained by strengthening her European ties, for Europe had her own expansionist dreams.

But Asia! Well, Asia was stretching herself with new beginnings, and whenever she felt like waving hello to new money, she always found herself waving at the USA across the Pacific. World War II brought an end to all such friendships for a few years, but even that could not stop the roll of new international relationships for long. The British Empire was breaking up, and the scattered national fragments of the old empire were eager to set up their own empires in which they could be sovereign. Having once been a part of that British Empire, America understood. Asia with her burgeoning population and self-confidence looked East, and California waved back.

A bridge opened in 1936 that was to wave a huge hello to all those immigrants who were sailing into California from the East. California grew strong! And America's old Europeans were amazed that the industrious Asian-Americans were bringing a kind of economic life to the twentieth century that the Gettys and Rockefellers had brought to the nineteenth. Never mind! America was open to everyone and big enough for everybody.

But California was soon to become the seedbed of all that was rapidly becoming America's biggest export business—entertainment. Hollywood would become even better known than some of the world's

largest cities. But shortly after that famous San Francisco bridge was built, an Iowan moved into southern California. His first name was Walt and he had a brother named Roy. Walt was the artist, and Roy was somewhat of an entrepreneur. There is a rumor of a legendary phone call that Walt made to Roy, asking if he could borrow a million dollars—quite a sum in those days. When Roy asked Walt why he wanted the money, Walt replied that he needed the money to finance a really great idea he had just had concerning a mouse and seven dwarfs. Walt ultimately entertained the world, but he wrote the word America in giant stars and stripes. And southern California made "America" look good, even at those times when Berkeley was making some Americans edgy.

They say that if you took California out of the fifty states and made it a nation all by itself that the wealthiest of nations would still be the remaining forty-nine states and that one of the wealthiest nations would be the new nation of California. California grew up all at once. It just sort of sprung up from a quaint string of Junipero Serra missions that stretched between San Juan Capistrano in the south and Mission Carmel in the north. That's about all of California that ever was quaint.

In some ways California never seemed to have its "country-church-and-town-hall" stage of growing up. Lots of people in the East sometimes felt California was unnecessary, and those in the Midwest thought it was too unrelated to God to ever have much to teach the rest of the nation. So it just sort of lay there, west of the Sierras, and, like most of the other states, wrote its own particular definition of what it means to be American.

NATIONAL PARKS

Teddy Roosevelt—that indomitable Rough Rider of the Spanish American War. Some said he was the brightest spot in the development of America. Teddy's love of the outdoors made a major gift to the people of America. He was the man who had decided that one of America's greatest resources was its natural beauty. Six years before I came to America, Katharine Lee Bates had written that poem that rapidly became everybody's sentiment; it must have been Roosevelt's too:

> O beautiful for spacious skies,
>
> For amber waves of grain,
>
> For purple mountain majesties
>
> Above the fruited plain.
>
> America! America!
>
> God shed His grace on thee!
>
> And crown thy good with brotherhood
>
> From sea to shining sea!

Well, Teddy Roosevelt decided to do something about making America's beauty accessible to everyone. That's how millions of acres of nature were marked off for all Americans to enjoy as national parks.

The National Park Act seemed to call out the best in America's artists. But it was in 1927 that a little known American artist, Gutzon Borglum, was to speak for all of us when he swung a scaffold over a pinnacle of granite in South Dakota. He spent the next thirteen years making the new national monument look committed to American heritage. When his glorious scaffolding was folded for the last time, four of America's greatest leaders stared out from a mountain. One of those faces was—yes, you guessed it—Theodore Roosevelt.

What motivates a man to carve a mountain? Well, he said that America had those kind of heroes that needed to be lifted so high that only the wind and the rain could wear them away. It's easy to cherish

a country whose citizens love her natural beauty. That's what the national parks all seem to say, "America is here to stay—to gaze at her magnificent wilderness beauty is to see her endurance."

God, not Borglum, is the real Sculptor of all of America's national parks. Gaze at the firm rock of Yosemite's El Capitan, and you will feel America's imperishable glory.

See the lonely monoliths of Canon Beach, and you will see the cleansing sea at prayer.

Hear the thunder of Yellowstone's waters.

Feel the spray of Niagara.

Stare at the white sands of New Mexico. All of it will say the national spirit is an anthem of pride.

We are Americans.

As enduring as Rushmore.

As strong as the Tetons.

As refreshing as the geysers of the West.

As vast as the Grand Canyon.

As raw as the prairies of Texas and the Everglades of Florida.

We are the land of purple mountain majesties above the fruited plains.

America, which has the most glorious present still existing in the world today, hardly stops to enjoy it, in her insatiable appetite for the future.[17]

ANNE MORROW LINDBERGH, *The Beach at My Back*

ADVERSITY

For eight decades now I have watched Americans stand together in times of adversity. World War I, Black Tuesday, the Great Depression, World War II, Vietnam, Watergate. Adversity seems to bring out all that's best about Americans. But perhaps the sense of common commitment was never any greater than when John F. Kennedy created a national consensus during the Cuban Missile Crisis in 1962. The youngest president ever to occupy the White House defied the Russians, demanding that they remove all the nuclear missiles from Cuba. Ultimately, the Russians backed down, and American togetherness triumphed.

Those were dark days indeed. Americans were told of the possible cost. The war with Russia had always been a cold one, and Kennedy was a valiant cold warrior. But now no one knew for sure whether the Russians would back down. A kind of anxiety—if not fear—fell upon America. But while Americans filled their larders with food for the possible coming conflict, they became instantly patriotic. People stored a reserve of fresh water, and some even built dugout bomb shelters; there was no major backlash of disloyalty.

But it was not so much the removal of the missiles that was noteworthy. It was the sense of solidarity that Americans represented in standing behind their youthful president. Americans, who can sometimes appear very partisan and divided, are capable of fierce togetherness when the occasion demands it. *E Pluribus Unum* has always been our motto and one we've always stood by when the occasion demanded.

But for individuals as for nations, it has always been true that adversity makes us stronger. For individuals or nations, where we trip is where the treasure lies. Those burdens that do not break us invariably make us stronger. God's grace washes cleanest those who did the right thing when they were most afraid.

Papa was old, but he believed in taking a stand even when the stakes were high. Papa said, "You know this crisis has been the one that's good

for America. Most of the crises we've faced as a nation we faced when some overseas tyrant made some threat. Then we all got together and sent people far away to solve the problem. But this time the enemy is right off the coast of Florida. This time the crisis could end in Washington or Memphis or Cedar Falls, for that matter."

We knew Papa was right.

We prayed. Most Americans just stayed together and prayed. We even met down at the church and took the whole matter to God. We prayed all that night, but it was Papa who prayed loudest:

"Lord, help the neighboring countries act like Christians, and above all help Christians to act like Christians. Help us to stand firm on the principle of courage and what's right. Best of all, Lord, we always looked to You when we didn't know how things were going to turn out. Guess this wouldn't be any time to stop doing that."

That was how Cedar Falls replied to the threat of nuclear war. Once the crisis was past, I guess we knew we'd done the right thing.

I believe in America because in it we are free—free to choose our government, to speak our minds, to observe our different religions.
Because we are generous with our freedoms, we share our rights with those who disagree with us,
Because we hate no people and covet no people's lands. Because we are blessed with a natural and varied abundance.
Because we have great dreams and because we have the opportunity to make those dreams come true.[18]

WENDELL LEWIS WILLKIE, *Epitaph*

FAITH

Americans have always been a people of faith. In the last half of the twentieth century, there has been quite an attempt to get prayer out of the American vocabulary. But the naysayers have not been able to root Americans from the kind of faith they learned in the hard times to practice in all times. Everywhere one looks there are clear indicators that Americans are people of faith. Presidents are sworn in on the Bible. Congress opens its sessions with prayer. The president proclaims a national day of prayer every year. The Supreme Court building is etched with the Ten Commandments. Thanksgiving is a holiday designated by the Congress of the United States. The First Amendment to the Constitution promises religious liberty.

But the God of Americans is not just the Father of Jesus; He is the keeper of that liberty which Americans so treasure. In virtually all of our national hymns, anthems, and pledges, God is seen as the Giver of liberty. When Americans rearranged "God Save the King" into the patriotic song "My Country 'Tis of Thee," it confessed God as the source of national greatness.

Our Father God to thee, Author of Liberty! To Thee we sing!

When Francis Scott Key wrote his now famous "Defense of Fort McHenry," he appealed to the sovereignty of God to guard America:

Oh! thus be it ever; when freemen shall stand

Between their loved homes and the war's desolation!

Blest with victory and peace, may the heaven-rescued land

Praise the Power that hath made and preserved us a nation.

Then conquer we must, when our cause it is just,

And this be our motto: "In God is our trust."

And the Star-Spangled banner forever shall wave.

Katherine Bates confessed in "America the Beautiful":

America, America, God shed His grace on thee,

And crowned thy good with brotherhood, from sea to shining sea.

Irving Berlin brought World War II alive with his stirring testament

to God's care of America:

> *God bless America, Land that I love,*
>
> *Stand beside her and guide her,*
>
> *Through the night with a light from above.*

America has many symbols—the flag, the eagle, the torch, the Capitol—but behind them all stands a faith grounded in God.

Maybe some people thought it a bit strange that I had the organist play "America the Beautiful" at Papa's funeral. He died in the spring of '66. "Son," he said to me just a few weeks before the fatal heart attack that took his life, "at my funeral I want you to tell them three things. First, tell them that the best Christians I ever knew were the ones I met with weekly in the Cedar Falls Church. Second, I want you to tell them that God was the best friend I ever had. And third, I want you to make it very clear that God shed His love on this great land, and they must never look slightingly on the land that God loved so much."

Well, I told them all Papa wanted them to know, though I broke down a couple of times in getting it out. The service wasn't long, and the processional was very short from the pulpit to the churchyard where Papa was laid to rest.

He had a modest stone set on his grave with only one phrase etched into the gray granite:

To your descendants I will give this land. Genesis 12:7

*The Americans have all a lively faith in the perfectibility of man, they judge that the diffusion of knowledge must necessarily
be advantageous and the consequences of ignorance, fatal; they all consider society as a body in a state of improvement, humanity as a changing scene, in which nothing is or
ought to be, permanent; and they admit that what appears to them today to be good, may be superceded by something better tomorrow.*[19]

ALEXIS DE TOCQUEVILLE, *Democracy in America*

THE OPTIMISTIC AMERICAN

Daniel Webster said that Americans are those people who hang out their signs indicating their respective trade. "Shoemakers hang out a gigantic shoe; jewelers, a monster watch; the dentist hangs out a gold tooth; but up in the mountains of New Hampshire, God Almighty has hung out a sign to show that there He makes men."[20]

It's sometimes hard to tell if God made Americans or if He just made America and America made Americans. Daniel Webster may in many ways be the archetype of all Americans. He remained so to the last. His final words were, "I still live!"[21] Of course, you've got to be alive to bear that kind of testimony. No dead man ever bragged about being alive. But the best part of his brag was that New Hampshirians were Americans. So are Pennsylvanians and Kansans. Isn't much of a trick to being an American. All you have to do is stay alive and be born somewhere between the Atlantic and Pacific and Canada and Mexico.

But the best Americans know that America is more than geography and

Americans are more than just inhabitants. Americans are those who can always say, "I still live, and thank God, I still live where every morning the quality of life I enjoy says I'm an American. I respect every man or woman in the world, but America is my address, and American is my pedigree."

Optimism is the mood of America. Anything is possible, everything attainable. "Little of beauty has America given the world save the rude grandeur of God Himself stamped on her bosom; the human spirit in this new world has expressed itself in vigor and ingenuity rather than in beauty."[22] The American recipes for success are all simple. When J. Paul Getty was asked his recipe for making millions, he said, "Get up early, work hard, find oil!"

Nothing is complicated about American optimism. It seems to work so often and so predictably that being an entrepreneur in some area of industry or the arts is a reasonable expectation. *It can be done* has the same number of syllables as *America*.

THE FIRST AMERICAN AND THE GREAT AMERICAN

The first Americans have awakened all of us immigrants to a new sense of honesty. They were here when Columbus thought he was discovering something new.

It was new to Europeans, but not to the Sioux or the Kiowa or the Anasazi. The various flags of an emerging republic came behind the hardy souls who walked America's pristine forests and plains.

In 1955 a young minister, Martin Luther King Jr., organized a boycott of some city bus lines in Alabama, and America once again was forced to widen her definitions of all that it meant to be American. Ever so slowly, we of European descent were forced to give up our narrower definitions of immigrant America and widen it forever to the greater end of national oneness.

Mark Twain was born when Halley's comet appeared in the nineteenth century and he swore he'd live till it appeared in the twentieth. He did what he swore, and from the time I first arrived in America, his wit and wisdom dominated American humor. In fact he barely got out of the way in time to give the stage to Will Rogers a decade later. But it was Twain who properly labeled America when he said, "We Americans are the lavishest and showiest and most luxury-loving people on the earth; and at our masthead we fly one true and honest symbol, the gaudiest flag the world has ever seen."[24]

Who can deny it? Every state gets a star and the first thirteen get both a star and a stripe. But isn't it grand? In all my years of watching America grow, I've never gotten tired of that grand and gaudy symbol. For its lavish colors suggest a wonderful racial inclusion of those who came against their will and those who were here before us. This national symbol is really a metaphor for the most colorful set of citizens the world has ever known. We were the melting pot nation, and in reality we didn't melt all that well. The variety of cultures has remained distinct: Germans, Japanese, Africans, Asians, and those who were here first. All of us have kept the word bland out of the national recipe for getting along together. But we've given the

world some huge lessons on how to get along inside our none-too-roomy national boundaries.

The recipe is to stir a thousand people groups together and teach each of them to love and cherish the differences. The flag wraps all America into a oneness that never forgets that each person is sovereign in the right to life, liberty, and the pursuit of happiness. For some the pursuit is easy, but everyone has a chance. In a world in which every new sunrise sees continuing wars of genocide, America remains the best example of respectful diversity. And as one of our great presidents said, "The world should always be safe for diversity." In fact, diversity should make the world rich.

No wonder Stephen Vincent Benét wrote,

American Muse, whose strong and diverse heart

So many men have tried to understand

But only made it smaller with their art,

Because you are as various as your land.[25]

We'll float the barge on the little river until it joins the bigger river.
And there where it joins the river to be, we'll float our way to the open sea.
And there at last on the open sea, we'll watch America come to be.[26]
CALVIN MILLER

AMERICA
THE RIVER RUNS THROUGH IT

Cedar Falls wasn't too far from the Mississippi River. The Mississippi cuts America into two wonderful halves, and both halves put together make America. They say that the Mississippi-Missouri basin is the third longest river in the world.

America has rugged coasts and scenic shores, but America has always been defined by the rivers that drain into the Mississippi the east side of the Rockies and into the Colorado and the Columbia on the west side of the Rockies.

The best thing about Cedar Falls is the Cedar River. You've never heard of it? Well, nobody is required in studying geography to know about the Cedar River. But it does make its contribution to the Mississippi basin, and without its little bit of water the Mighty Miss would be a little lower, near St. Louis.

The Cedar River is a little river with a set of rapids that got labeled Cedar Falls. But in the spring when the trout wake up hungry, they'll bite at even the smallest hunk of feathers, just as though it were a well-tied lure. I used to take my boys there, and we'd try to forget about what the thirties were doing to all American farmers. Back before the farmers got citified and started playing golf, they all used to fish. I'm not saying you can't get away from it all by playing golf, but I'm here to tell you that even the best golfers might find just a little bit of therapy in learning how to tie up a fly with a little brass hook designed to land in the jaw of three-pound rainbow trout.

Somehow, the whole thing is just plain American—standing there with a supple rod, whipping it lightly into a frenzy while the string waves outward from a smooth reel till you've got yourself a hundred feet of "esses" flying overhead. Then the snap and the release and the slow draw of a small clot of quail-down, moving slowly across the water. Then the hungry fish jumps on your line and flies in a fury while you let him go till he thinks he's free, and you bring him back again while his fiery skin flicks color at the afternoon sun. Again and again, he runs for the shady logs, and again and again he turns to honor the tension in the line, till there he is—snuggled in with his peers who have

also lost to the silver line—inside your creel.

But somehow it was never the Cedar River that helped me deal with the stress of the "Dirty Thirties", as "Okies" sometimes referred to the depression. It was Cedar Creek that fed the Cedar River so it could feed the Mississippi. No flies and swaling on the creek. No silver cord on Cedar Creek. There on the creek with a "Clabber-Girl" can of worms and a rusty tackle box, a man could hope for an unlucky catfish while he watched for water moccasins. Never liked those moccasins 'cause they could unhinge their ugly jaws and swallow the biggest fish on the stringer. But worse than that they were so aggressive that they'd come after you personally if you had something they wanted.

Most of the time on a creek bank I'd watch the foam bubbles and dragonflies, and I'd fish. I liked fishing alone, because there'd be no one there to contest the stories I'd later tell. I was a typical fisherman in some ways. The one that got away was always the biggest one of all, and it always got larger with the telling. But somehow there on the bank, I'd get to talking to God, just like

He was a Lutheran and we were sitting in church. And God would remind me that creek banks were the best part of America, and there a man and his Maker could figure out just what it would take to make the world sane once again.

And, above all, I'd listen hard to God. Because you never get God properly served until you shut up and let Him do the talking. And most of the time, after a long day, we'd just keep talking till Hildy had floured and fried the best eating Cedar Creek could produce. And somehow if there was enough chopped onion in the hush puppies, it made for Thanksgiving in August and a season of high worship at mealtime, especially if there were fried green tomatoes on the side.

It was the little things like this that made even creek banks places where you knew that the Dirty Thirties were temporary. There was too much abundance swimming in Cedar Creek to doubt that the rest of the United States wasn't just as full of it. It wouldn't be long till God would set the economy back on its feet, and the whole nation would honor the private prayers of fishermen.

When Tillage begins, other arts follow. The Farmers therefore are the founders of human civilization.[27]

DANIEL WEBSTER

FARMS

AMERICA'S GIFT TO ITSELF

It was in the late thirties that I found the greatest joy any farmer in those days could know: a John Deere tractor. One could only imagine the revolution that was about to occur. I always wondered how Goliath and Mary—our faithful old Clydesdales—felt about that infernal green machine that Papa drove down the road with its cast-steel lugs, biting into the red roads like a dragon eating shale.

But whatever Goliath and Mary thought, I was immediately in love with that heavy green tractor. First of all it could pull a two-bottomed plow and never strain. And I never had to yell "Gee" or "Haw" at the corners of the field. Ah, but the best part was that I could ride, and I never had to get off of the plow seat to feed or water the team.

But whether I was on the "Poppin' Johnny," as we called the tractor, or whether I was riding the rolling plow with the team, farming was the way I measured what I was getting done. There was something glorious in watching a plow turn the chocolate earth. It was the good feeling that came from being a partner with God until you were worn out with the sun and sweat of the partnership.

Farming was like fishing. It was a job you did alone. It was a way a man found God and always found God ready for a conversation. Farming was like working inside a cinema with a thousand pictures all around you of the faithfulness of God. It was easy to see God in the birth of a new calf or in the lightning over your own fields. It was a time to reckon with God when there was too much rain or too little. There was the fear of a short harvest or of the grain going down in a soggy July. There was the never-ending need to shingle the outbuildings or paint the main place. There were chickens to fry and apricots to can and melons to pack in the oat straw of August.

But autumn is the farmer's season. It's when the frost comes to kill the pollen in the air and coat the pumpkins. Autumn is the last reminder that it's time to get into the thickets and pick out the dead

trees for firewood. Autumn reminds us that there under the cellar door is stashed away half a thousand jars of green beans and black-eyed peas, and six orange crates of the biggest potatoes to be saved. Of course that was all Hildegard's work, and she never failed to do her garden-farming while God and I made corn together. On top of the old weathered pine of the cellar door were enough pumpkins to last till January. There would be pies enough for all the church dinners and hot bread for the big snow days that were just around the corner.

Yet it wasn't how much produce we had gotten together by November that made farming the right way to live. It was the land itself and how you met God at the end of every corn row or the beginning of the soybean field. Farming was its own reward, and the reward was directly from God. Psalms 14:1 says, "The fool has said in his heart, / 'There is no God,'" and of course other thinkers have always had other opinions on the matter. But I used to rephrase Psalms 14:1 to say, "No farmer ever said in his heart, 'There is no God.'" Farmers just plain know better. Because when you stand in the middle of a hundred-acre field and realize that only God could ever make it bring forth a single ear of corn, you know you're in a needy relationship with God. That's the blessing of the farmer's life. God is never luxury, always necessity.

Sometime when the granary was full, and the silo was gorged with the faithfulness of God, I'd bless God for autumn. But if it had been a bad year, I never found it in my heart to blame God. The truth was I had to trust Him and wait and believe that in the good times God was God and in the bad times He was still God. It was then that I'd look at the silo, knowing that there wasn't enough stuff there, especially if the winter was long. It was then that I'd read some words from the Old Testament:

Though the fig tree does not bud and there are no grapes on the vines,

though the olive crop fails and the fields produce no food,

though there are no sheep in the pen and no cattle in the stalls,

yet I will rejoice in the LORD,

I will be joyful in God my Savior. (Hab. 3:17–18 NIV)

God wants a faith that waits on rain and believes when the ground is dry. The miracles that miss us on Monday will surely come on Tuesday. Next year's abundance is attached to this year's need by our willingness to trust in God.

THE FINAL DAYS OF JEAN PIERRE GODET

WRITTEN BY HIS SON, WILLIAM WALTON GODET

Today I laid my father, Jean Pierre Godet, to rest in the Lutheran churchyard. He died April 4, 1985, at the age of 92 years. My father was born in Europe but never called Europe his home. His home held that adopted high-esteem that only one's freely chosen citizenship can afford. Being born in Belgium was not his to choose. But becoming an American was a choice he made with gratitude toward God. As an American veteran he had long let it be known to his family that he wanted a military funeral. His flag-draped casket at the cemetery waited on a twenty-one gun salute and the playing of taps. He had earlier requested that only two pieces of material be read at his funeral. The first was the Twenty-third Psalm, and the second was a letter that my grandfather had written to his aging sister in Belgium.

The letter we found among his papers in a tin box under his bed. The text of the letter ran as follows:

To My Beloved Sister, Katharine,

Today is November 3, 1917, and Jean Pierre was sworn into the infantry of the U.S. Army. Since my dearest Ermagarde died, John Pierre is all that I have left. I cannot tell you the mixed sense of joy and pain I have felt upon his leaving for the war. I cannot withhold Jean Pierre and forbid him to take part in the army, for the importance of this war is hard to estimate. I feel a strange contradiction between my love for Jean Pierre and my love for America. It is difficult to surrender my son that my country may be free. On the other hand, without the willingness of all Americans to make these kinds of sacrifices neither the country nor the world would long remain free.

So, I am alone, and my son too is alone. I only pray that all Americans whenever they are called upon to make such sacrifices will make them with courage, fully aware of the possible cost. For now my new loneliness has left me melancholy. I cannot see the flag above the courthouse without feeling a grip in my stomach. I cannot see a man in uniform without seeing my own beloved son, framed in the center of my

heart. I pray daily that he will live and the war will be short.

In the meantime I remember that the Good Book says "Righteousness exalteth a nation." I only pray that all Americans will desire to live the good life and seek to make their actions pleasing to God.

There are a few lines in our national anthem that remind me of all that Jean Pierre and I have felt as we hugged good-bye at the train station:

Oh, thus be it ever, when free men shall stand

Between their loved homes and the war's desolation;

Blest with vict'ry and peace, may the heaven rescued land

Praise the pow'r that hath made and preserved us a nation!

I live with these words blazing through my hopes. I daily pray for my son to come home from the war and soon.

But I cannot resent America for all that she has demanded of our family during these days of pain and sacrifice. Rather, I love America for giving so many of us the right to dream a new dream. I love America for opening her lands to the plows of hopeful immigrants like me. I love America for being a land where a man and woman can serve God and bring their children up according to the dictates of their own hearts. I love America, and when Jean Pierre has come marching home, I hope to hold his sons on my lap and tell them of the glories of this good land in which they came to be born. I pray the Lord will make it our heritage forever."

I finished the letter. Then far across the cemetery came the lonely report of the rifles: twenty-one volleys from ricocheting rifles. And following that, the lonely, clear call of a bugle, whose golden throat said to all, "Jean Pierre Godet was an American." He loved the family God gave him and the rich land God gave him in which to raise his family.

The cadets took the flag from the casket, folded it into a triangle of pride, and presented it to my aging mother. We walked back into the Lutheran church. We had a great Cedar Falls dinner, topped off with apple pie. One of the Brunt girls had made those pies from the apples she had canned back in the fall. They were apples that came from those graftings once carried across the Atlantic in Grandpa Godet's steamer trunk.

I just couldn't help but remember what Grandpa Godet said after one of those same great pies earlier in his life: "Well, could use a tad more cinnamon, to my way of thinking. Still, apple trees express the nation's best optimism. When you plant a good apple tree in a good land, you secure dessert well into the next century."

NOTES

1. Mary Antin, taken from *John Bartlett Familiar Quotations*, Emily Morison Beck (Boston: Little, Brown, 1968), 963.

2. James Baldwin, taken from Rhonda Thomas Tripp, comp., *The International Thesaurus of Quotations* (New York: Thomas Y. Crowell, 1970), 19.

3. Woodrow Wilson, taken from Bartlett, *Quotations*, 842.

4. Edgar Z. Friedenberg, taken from Tripp, *Thesaurus*, 20.

5. Lyndon B. Johnson, taken from Tripp, *Thesaurus*, 20.

6. "John Henry," an American folk ballad.

7. John F. Kennedy, taken from Tripp, *Thesaurus*, 20.

8. Jacques Maritain, taken from Tripp, *Thesaurus*, 20.

9. James Bryant Conant, taken from Bartlett, *Quotations*, 1026.

10. Padraic Colum

11. Alexis de Tocqueville, taken from Bartlett, *Quotations*, 616.

12. Walt Whitman, taken from Bartlett, *Quotations*, 699.

13. Henry Cabot Lodge, taken from Bartlett, *Quotations*, 821.

14. Stephen Vincent Benét, taken from Bartlett, *Quotations*, 1041.

15. Daniel Webster, taken from Bartlett, *Quotations*, 548.

16. Woodrow Wilson, taken from Tripp, *Thesaurus*, 23.

17. Anne Morrow Lindbergh, taken from Tripp, *Thesaurus*, 21.

18. Wendell Lewis Willkie, taken from Bartlett, *Quotations*, 1025.

19. Alexis de Tocqueville, taken from Bartlett, *Quotations*, 616.

20. Daniel Webster, taken from Bartlett, *Quotations*, 548.

21. Ibid.

22. W. E. B. Du Bois, taken from Tripp, *Thesaurus*, 20.

23. Wendell Lewis Willkie, taken from Bartlett, *Quotations*, 1025.

24. Mark Twain, taken from Tripp, *Thesaurus*, 22.

25. Stephen Vincent Benét, taken from Bartlett, *Quotations*, 1041.

26. Calvin Miller.

27. Daniel Webster, taken from Bartlett, Quotations, 548.

28. Max Lerner, taken from Tripp, *Thesaurus*, 19.